John Kenneth Galbraith

Already known as an economist, essayist, and novelist, Mr. Galbraith began experimenting two years ago with the political tract. His **How to Get Out of Vietnam** ***(1968) and*** **How to Control the Military** ***(1969), are widely credited with changing and shaping ideas on two problems of great importance to every concerned American.***

Mr. Galbraith was born in Canada and educated there and in the United States. During World War II, he was in charge of wartime price control in Washington, was on the staff of Adlai Stevenson in 1952 and 1956, and served during the Kennedy Administration both as presidential adviser and as ambassador to India. He was an early and influential supporter of Senator Eugene McCarthy and seconded his nomination at the Democratic Convention of 1968. Mr. Galbraith is considered one of the most important contemporary economists, and his writings in this field, including *The New Industrial State* and *The Affluent Society*, are regarded as landmark works on the economics of modern life. John Kenneth Galbraith is presently the Paul M. Warburg Professor of Economics at Harvard.

Other Signet Broadsides
by John Kenneth Galbraith

HOW TO GET OUT OF VIETNAM	S3414—35¢
HOW TO CONTROL THE MILITARY	P4019—60¢

Who Needs the Democrats

and What It Takes to Be Needed

JOHN KENNETH GALBRAITH

A SIGNET BROADSIDE from
NEW AMERICAN LIBRARY
TIMES MIRROR

Library of Congress Catalog Card Number: 77-125291

This is an authorized reprint of a hardcover edition published by
Doubleday & Company, Inc.

SIGNET TRADEMARK REG. U.S. PAT. OFF. AND FOREIGN COUNTRIES
REGISTERED TRADEMARK—MARCA REGISTRADA
HECHO EN CHICAGO, U.S.A.

SIGNET, SIGNET CLASSICS, MENTOR AND PLUME BOOKS
are published by The New American Library, Inc.,
1301 Avenue of the Americas, New York, New York 10019

FIRST PRINTING, AUGUST, 1970

PRINTED IN THE UNITED STATES OF AMERICA

FOR

BROOKS BECK AND JOSEPH L. RAUH, JR.

PERSONAL PROTECTOR AND

PUBLIC DEFENDER

Who Needs the Democrats

and What It Takes to be Needed

FOREWORD

For thirty-odd years I have been a reasonably active Democrat, and over all that time my relations with the Party have varied from uneasy to unpleasant. In the late thirties, the Party elders in Washington viewed the evangelistic young Keynesians who were around town with distaste and even alarm. I was one. Later, when in charge of wartime price control, I was thought, along with Leon Henderson, to have caused the loss of a number of key congressional seats in 1942. (In politics one only loses key seats, never non-key seats.) I have always felt that the contention had merit. So did F.D.R., who a few months later dispensed with my services to general applause. He offered me a job in South Africa. In 1952, the people who were helping Adlai Stevenson on economic policy were felt by more reputable Democrats to be guiding him too far to the left—a view that was shared by Adlai himself. Again I was one. Later, during the Eisenhower years, I was chairman of the domestic policy committee of the Democratic Advisory Council. For the first time in Party affairs, I found myself burdened by the responsible position. Accordingly I was assailed by Leon Keyserling from left and right and Dean Acheson from the right. (Dean and I clashed also on foreign policy.

At the time he was persuaded that John Foster Dulles was being too soft on the Communists.) In the early sixties, I found myself in disagreement with my old Keynesian allies over tax reduction. Such a reduction was required by what was now the new orthodoxy. I thought the money should be used for public needs. Nothing serves one so well in politics as the ability to change sides. Consistency is what freezes you to error. For several months in the late sixties, the Massachusetts State Committee met only to consider my ejection from a highly symbolic Party post. Fortunately the matter never came to a vote. Vietnam was by now the issue. Prior to the Chicago Convention, a move to expunge me from the delegation for the same heresy did succeed. The first order of business before the delegation when it caucused at Chicago was a resolution to remove me again, for meanwhile I had arrived back on. One could, eventually, get the feeling of not being wanted.

None of this is to establish my right to a persecution complex or even my credentials as an excessively experienced malcontent. It merely allows me to point out the most important thing about the Democratic Party, which is that no matter how much you may dislike it and vice versa, you cannot escape it. And the reason is the *raison d'être* of the Party. The Democratic Party, not the Republican Party, not third parties, is where change occurs and thus where the action is. This follows, in turn, from the deepest political instinct of the American people. It is this instinct that the natural access to political influence by those with a grievance is through the Democrats. It is the party that is open to participation and responsive to pressure. This instinct, during the last century, brought the successive waves of poorer immigrants—Irish, Italians, Jews—into the Democratic Party. It brought the alliance with the unions. It is what, astonishingly, made Democrats of black Americans when they moved north to escape the rigor and repression of life under the Democrats in the South. It was what, in 1968, caused the young to rally to the city and party of Richard Daley, rather than to Miami Beach. Even the alienated when they get alienated get alienated from the Democrats, not the Republicans.

The difference between the two parties, a more considerable one than cliché commonly allows, is here. The Republicans on the whole enroll those who value what is or was. Their leaders accept change tactically or defensively and with an eye on the Democrats. The Democratic Party enrolls those who want change, usually for themselves. Leaders respond not with an eye to the Republicans, but with an eye to their followers.

And sometimes they are slow to respond. In the last few years, quite a few members of the Party have spent more time in regretting the unwise and importunate pressures of radicals and the young than in seeking to understand them. This pre-eminently was the mood of those who nominated Hubert Humphrey at Chicago in 1968. ("We won the nomination without the kids," one of his acolytes said afterward, "and we will win the election without them." He was half right.) Men who were once stalwart liberals are often the slowest to respond; they righteously celebrate their association with past revolutions that have since become old hat as, alas, they do not see.

The highly imperfect response of the Democratic Party to the world as it has become, along with the remedy, are the concern of this small book. Some are bound to ask if it is worthwhile. I hope so. Its shortcomings, eccentricities and anachronisms notwithstanding, the Democratic Party has been the instrument of a remarkable amount of change from the days of the New Deal on. I would hope it can be so again. In any case, there isn't anything else.

I

CONSERVATISM BY ATTRITION

EARLY LAST WINTER, about the time the Congress reassembled, I chanced to be relying for political wisdom on the *International Herald Tribune*, an excellent paper which saves you from the unimportant news and has an alarming collation of columnists. One day Joseph Alsop had an epistle from the Pentagon; the generals were conceiving a new missile gap and Joe was already several months pregnant. All the rest reflected on the poor condition of the Democratic Party.[1]

It was depressing. Most of the concern was with the leadership. Hubert was Hubert. Ted Kennedy had suffered a terrible misfortune which all regretted in the manner of the late Uriah Heep. (His political demise was, I thought, being celebrated a bit prematurely.) George McGovern was a sensible man, right on issues and notably so on the Vietnam war. But being right, he was therefore too unexciting. Harold Hughes hadn't

[1] None specified what that was, which was to evade a hard question. Here I have reference, broadly, to those who hold office under its entitlement and, as regards policy, to what was urged in the last election or now wins the support of a majority of the congressional party. Strictly from the administrative point of view, Paul Porter, the noted attorney, once said, the Democratic Party can be compared only to a house of casual pleasure run by the girls.

yet surfaced. Ed Muskie was generally praised for making no waves, not annoying anyone. But a man can stand only so much of that kind of praise.

The position of the Party in the House of Representatives was thought to be especially bad. John McCormack, the Pericles of progressive democracy in that not excessively august body, was held at seventy-eight to be unappealing to the very young. They *are* getting hard to please. His cronies, who had been using his office (so it is averred) to soften the impact of the impersonal state on their friends for a price, were thought to be unappealing to people of all ages. However, their operations had left the Democrats with no alternative next January but to re-elect old John in order to vindicate him and, generally speaking, show their appreciation. Carl Albert, the Majority Leader, was not considered a catalytic figure as, being a sensible man, he would not dream of regarding himself. Hale Boggs of Louisiana was not thought to be a man to capture the heart and mind of the masses in the ghetto. Members of the southern mandarinate in the House—Mendel Rivers of South Carolina, Jamie Whitten of Mississippi, William Colmer of the same precinct, Otto Passman of Louisiana—made Boggs look like the new Martin Luther King.

Nor could anything be done about it. Tradition dictates that however incompetent, unpopular or generally lousy the Democratic congressional leadership, it must, like the Union, be preserved. That is the American way. (In the Senate the Party position is not perfect. But there a score or more of sensitive, energetic liberals make it much better.)

There was also a great deal of hand-wringing over the debts of the Democrats from the last election, which the poets took seriously. No one else should. Most of this is owed to fat cats, some thick with lard, who put up the money with something more for themselves in mind than honest usury, if only a nice welcome at the White House. Humphrey lost and so did they. I was surprised, though, that none of my learned friends thought to dwell on the position of the Democrats in the great industrial states. These erstwhile strongholds —New York, Pennsylvania, New Jersey, Massachusetts, Minnesota, Michigan, as well as Ohio, Illinois and California—are all without exception governed or anyhow administered by Republicans. It is impossible to think of a Democratic governor of distinction and there could be a reason. Everything considered, if the test of the success of a party is the quality and number of its officeholders, the Democrats are not doing well.

2

The function of the columnists is to think for us, which is a great service and one that should be respected. But like others they assign too much importance to a sudden dystrophy of the Democratic leadership. There is, I think, a deeper cause, which is that the Democratic Party, within a relatively short span of time, has lost its main purposes. It has become a defender of the status quo, a role in which it is incompetent and cannot possibly compete with the Republicans. Harry Truman pointed out many years ago that faced with a choice between two conservative parties, the voters will always opt for the real thing.

History, in fact, has played a nasty trick on the Democrats. It has made politically commonplace all of the major policies for which the Party has stood in the last thirty years. The one important exception is its foreign policy, which it has made aggressively damaging. The men who occupy the positions of power and influence in the Party (with some notable exceptions) are still deeply committed to these policies or deeply identified with their own past. So, to borrow General Westmoreland's best word, they have become conservatives by attrition. Not that many would admit it. Being a liberal is like being an Episcopalian: If you have once been well and truly confirmed, you are allowed to consider yourself a communicant for life. You don't have to practice. But let me be specific.

3

In the thirty-odd years since Roosevelt and the peacetime New Deal, the national Democratic Party has won elections on five major policies. And the spillover from these policies won a legion of local contests. The policies were:

(1) Implementation of the New (or Keynesian) economics. This ensured, as all liberal Democrats believed, that the economic system worked.

(2) The elaboration of the Welfare State. This won the gratitude of all who because of age, sex, dependency, illness or the absence of a job could not make a go of it in the economic system.

(3) Support to the trade union movement. This got the unions.

(4) A reasonably firm if highly gradualist approach to the elimination of racial inequality. This got the voting blacks.

(5) A foreign and military policy which recognized our responsibilities as a superpower and more especially

as a bulwark (as we called it) against international Communism, and which armed ourselves and our allies accordingly, but which resisted the idea of solving delicate international problems by blowing everyone up. This appealed to the informed and substantial citizen.

This was not the whole agenda. There was a heavy payoff to the farmers. Support to education played an increasing role. In later years there was the poverty program and a mélange of efforts on behalf of the cities. But the five policies listed provided, I would think, some 90 per cent of the Democratic appeal. And, as noted, they won a great many elections. All have now gone down the drain, as a quick glance will suggest.

4

Apart from foreign policy, which is in a class by itself, the greatest misfortune of the Democrats has been in economics. It was long the deepest Democratic conviction that, in contrast with the pre-Keynesian and pre-Cambrian policies of the Republicans, they could manage the economy. Principally required was a modern or Keynesian economic policy—essentially the regulation of the total demand for economic product by the deliberate adjustment of Federal spending and taxation as well as of investment from borrowed funds. There is, in fact, little doubt that, by these methods, serious depression can be elided. But we now also know that it brings inflation. The single-minded concentration on production also brings a very unequal array of productive blessings—numerous automobiles, terrible housing—and is itself the cause of a disenchanting array of new disorders, of which environmental damage is currently inspiring the most oratory. And on these problems, alas, the Democrats are not identified with solutions. And to make matters worse, the Republicans have now adopted Keynes. Mr. Nixon's economists, some secondary distinctions between fiscal and monetary policy apart, are orthodox members of the Keynesian faith.

On the Welfare State, the Republicans have moved ahead of the Democrats. For years whenever Democratic scholars (a subcaste to which undubitably I belonged) told themselves they needed new ideas, they invariably had in mind some new and compelling form of social security—something like unemployment compensation or old age insurance that the voters would cherish and the Republicans would reliably oppose.

Actually the available ideas are far fewer than conservatives imagine. And the only important one in the last quarter century is the guaranteed minimum income. This makes money available to all who need it without a means test. Some part is given up as other income is earned, but in such fashion that a family never has less money as a result of a member getting a job. This idea unquestionably belongs to the Republicans. The guaranteed income, in a variant called the negative income tax, was first influentially broached by Professor Milton Friedman of the University of Chicago, once an adviser (so described anyhow) to Barry Goldwater. Except where monetary policy is involved, Professor Friedman, a man of highly independent mind, is not reliably wrong or even conservative. Liberal economists, most notably James Tobin, who was one of President Kennedy's economic advisers, have improved the idea. But it was President Nixon who proposed it to Congress. Though the rate suggested—$1600 for a family of four—is derisory, the political authorship of the idea is not in doubt.

Organized labor is still in alliance with the Democrats. It can still hold the big battalions as they did for Hubert Humphrey. But apart from a few progressive internationals the leadership is geriatric and sometimes, as in the case of the miners, repellent. Many of the leaders are archaically hardline on Communism, unapologetically for the Vietnam war and untroubled by the military power. In other words they are indifferent or hostile to what most concerns the younger Party members. In Massachusetts the McCarthy-Kennedy Democrats have recently been organizing to unseat Philip Philbin, an ancient timeserver from a district near Boston who as number two man on the House Armed Services Committee faithfully follows because he cannot anticipate every wish of the Pentagon and Mendel Rivers. A few months ago, I voiced general support for their enlightened effort. The first protest to arrive came from my friends in the state AFL-CIO. Philbin is right on labor.

Whatever the black community may be, it certainly isn't Republican. But here too there are nasty problems. When the Democrats do not have the White House, the southeners in Congress are exceedingly visible. This does not enhance the Party image in Bedford-Stuyvesant. Without the presidency there is no chance of offsetting this effect with a strong legislative initiative on civil rights. And legislative gradualism, which is what the Democrats have offered in the past, has lost much of its appeal to the blacks. They, not surprisingly, want equality now or soon and there isn't much sign of a Democratic formula for that. So all the Democrats have is Attorney General John Mitchell. It is theologically indefensible for a Democrat to pray for his health on purely political grounds. But some do.

Foreign policy is, of course, the crowning blow. The Democrats were supposed to be expert, intelligent and responsible in foreign affairs. They managed to come up with the worst disaster since the Civil War. The magnitude of the reaction to that disaster is still hard to appreciate. It is also hard to be other than proud. For the first time in modern history a great nation reacted to the unwisdom of a war in the middle of the war—not, as usually happens, after it is over. And, in effect, it threw the men who were responsible out. But the men responsible were Democrats or, more precisely, they had been given power by the Democrats. And the Democrats have been in office for every war since the skirmish with Spain. To those wars that were just or unavoidable, we have responsibility for one that no viable Democratic leader would now dream of defending.

Economics, foreign policy, the split in the Party as it relates to racial equality and some resulting questions of political style all require a special word. To these matters I now turn.

II

THE PROBLEM OF ECONOMIC POLICY

> "I am convinced that the success of our economy, which is the world's greatest success story, has had a tremendous impact on our enemies as well as our friends."
>
> Hubert H. Humphrey
> April 26, 1966

SOME YEARS AGO, in a considerable access of originality, Democratic presidential candidates stopped running against Herbert Hoover and the Great Depression. Possibly it was unwise, an impractical as well as unaccustomed concession to the young, for no other issue ever served the Party so well and to this day the polls show that the Democrats are thought better than the Republicans for putting down depression and unemployment. In the Roosevelt and Truman years the Democrats had a near monopoly of the notion that, by vigorous intervention in the economy—spending and a deficit when needed to overcome unemployment and sluggish performance, a surplus when inflation threatened—the economy could be made to work. The

Republicans cooperated admirably on all public occasions by reverently demanding a balanced budget, which was the one course of action that by nature excluded an effective economic policy.

The Eisenhower years, when nothing terrible happened, partly redeemed the Republicans from Hoover. But during much of the fifties there was a persistent and damaging increase in industrial prices, and by the end of the decade unemployment was above 6 per cent and economic growth negligible. Kennedy ran in 1960 on the promise "to get this country moving again," by which he meant a higher rate of economic expansion, a lower level of unemployment with, hopefully, a lesser rate of inflation. Remarkably enough as political promises go, he accomplished these things and added further to the reputation of the Democrats for good economic management.

It was a further tenet of the Democratic faith (and still it) that if unemployment was small and economic growth was adequate, the economic system worked. Fear of unemployment was the overwhelming psychic legacy of the Great Depression. Then upwards of a third of the working force was without jobs, and in the public and political mind, unemployment established itself as the one and transcendent domestic disaster. In principle the economic system was subject to tests of performance other than growth and jobs. In practice nothing else really counted. If the economic system worked, the system worked. In what he may well have considered an understatement, Lyndon Johnson summarized the Democratic achievement in his last economic report to the Congress.

> *The Nation is now in its 95th month of continuous economic advance. Both in strength and length, this prosperity is without parallel in our*

history. We have steered clear of the business-cycle recessions which for generations derailed us repeatedly from the path of growth and progress.

This record demonstrates the vitality of a free economy and its capacity for steady growth. No longer do we view our economic life as a relentless tide of ups and downs. No longer do we fear that automation and technical progress will rob workers of jobs rather than help us to achieve greater abundance. No longer do we consider poverty and unemployment permanent landmarks on our economic scene.

But it is no longer only the Democrats who can command such miracles. The Republicans are in principle equally apt—as some Democrats concede. Arthur Okun, the last Chairman of the Council of Economic Advisers under the Democrats, recently observed that: "The bipartisan nature of our national commitment to full prosperity was clearly demonstrated in the initial months of the Nixon administration. This was the most significant and gratifying development in economic policy in 1969."[2]

The Republicans have also discovered that the bipartisan commitment to posterity has some significant but less gratifying features. On these, Lyndon Johnson, like other members of his party, was not so inclined to dwell.

[2] Arthur M. Okun. *The Political Economy of Prosperity.* New York. W. W. Norton, 1970. p. 123.

2

The formula for ensuring "the vitality of a free economy" is to encourage more public and private spending when the economy is slack, including more borrowing and investment from borrowed funds. And when inflation is the problem, the process is reversed. The Republicans set particular store by raising interest rates to cut back on spending from borrowed funds—the tight-money policy—but this is difference of method within the larger strategy.

The difficulty is that strong unions and powerful corporations can defeat the policy by raising wages and prices whenever the economy is close to full employment. And the prices so raised are passed along to the rest of the economy—to postal employees and airline controllers and civil servants generally—forcing compensatory wage increases even by the government itself. This is what has happened in recent months. Thus while employment remains high inflation continues.

If the cutback in demand is big enough, there will come a point when prices cannot be raised. But by this time there will be a good deal of unemployment (and some other strains which I will mention in a moment) with the result that the remedy will seem worse than the inflation that it cures, especially for those who, for the larger public good, are righteously deprived of their jobs and stock market gains.

The Republicans have lately been risking this remedy. So far they have managed to combine a modest reduction in growth and employment with the highest rate of inflation in twenty years. Their economists continue to promise stability. But such promises have been made week by week and month by month for a year and a half. Even economists are expected some day to make good. (Only in foreign policy is one allowed to say that failure is success.) And there has now been a tacit confession of failure. The tight money punishes with peculiar severity the smaller businessman, who must borrow money, while leaving comparatively untroubled the large corporation, which has its own resources and, in any case, is a favored client of the banks. The housing industry is a particular casualty of the policy. These consequences forced some easing off, even while consumer prices were rising at a near record rate.

The obvious solution is to intervene directly to limit the wage and price increases that are the causative factor. Under similar circumstances other industrial countries do so as have we in the past. But this encounters deep moral objections—it is a confession in effect that the free-price system, the Holy Grail of all good Republicans and of all economists who yearn for respectability, no longer functions as it is supposed to do. It means that the corporations in conjunction with the unions have too much market power. This is a terrible thing for a good Republican or an economist who cherishes his reputability to have to believe. (A further and compelling objection for some economists is that it means conceding that the Galbraith line on these matters is right.)

In the early Kennedy-Johnson years, the Democrats experimented with wage-price restraints—the so-called guideposts. They worked well for a time but succumbed under the pressure of the Vietnam war. Since then, Democrats have been almost as reluctant as Republicans to come to grips with the inflation problem. Talk of wage and price control is poorly regarded by the

Establishment. Democrats yearn to be reputable too. Mr. Gardner Ackley, who preceded Arthur Okun as head of the Council of Economic Advisers and whom Hubert Humphrey recently named head of the Economic Policy Committee of the new Democratic Council, tolerantly told the Republicans last winter that he didn't blame them for avoiding such action.

3

There are other economic problems that the Democrats have been reluctant to face: The Keynesian economy relies to a disconcerting degree on military expenditures. These, amounting to about half of all Federal expenditure in recent years, provide a highly reliable flow of demand to the private economy. Meanwhile the taxes that support this expenditure are flexible —they rise when production, profits and other incomes rise and thus exercise a dampening effect and increase less rapidly or fall when production and incomes fall, thus releasing revenues for private spending.

Liberal Democrats, over the years, have developed a singular faculty for closing their eyes to the role so played by military outlays. It was the by-product of cold-war necessity and purely an accident that it helped the economy. Civilian spending would do just as well and would be welcomed as an alternative by every decent citizen.

By now it is clear that we get military appropriations far more easily than civilian ones. A budget-conscious congressman is (or was until recently) a man who wanted to cut back on nonmilitary spending. Military spending is also the cover for extensive socialization of technological development where that is too expensive or too risky for private enterprise to pay for itself. Atomic energy, the computer, modern air transport all have been so aided. And a new and uncouth generation is pointing these things out.

Yet, by and large, the political liturgy has not come abreast. In the cold-war years Democrats, liberals especially, were required to praise the economic system on all occasions of public ceremony and celebration. It was how one proved he was a Keynesian and for the Welfare State without being a Communist. The old music continues. It is still a basic assumption that subject to some tinkering, the system works. As long as it depends on big arms outlays for stabilization and technical dynamic it does not work, and the oratory which so holds has a patently fraudulent sound.

4

The system is gravely deficient in two other respects. Its performance is highly uneven. In about half the economy—that half characterized by the large corporations or where needs of the large corporations are being served—production is efficient, men are well paid, for those that belong there is no poverty. In consequence our supply of automobiles, gasoline, highways, household appliances, detergents, gargles, space vehicles and weaponry is excellent. Outside of the world of the large corporation the performance is far less reliable—or satisfactory. This is especially true of that part of the economy which makes urban life agreeable or even tolerable. Housing, surface transportation, hospital and health services, street cleaning, police services and the courts, other municipal services and education are provided with increasing relative and often with increasing absolute inefficiency. And poor productive performance in this part of the economy is matched by poor employment conditions. Jobs are poorly paid and vulnerable (as in the case of public employees) to inflation. In further consequence of this and other factors, income inequality is increasing. Thus, although national income and gross product continue to rise, they disguise an increasingly disparate performance within the economy. And it is from the disparity that the urban dweller and especially the urban ghetto dweller suffers. He has to live with the fact of the poor performance and the poor wages it pays. He cannot be told that the system works.

But a heavy indirect price is also exacted where it does work. Production rises but the price of increasing production is unpleasant and even lethal surroundings. The air is less breathable, the water less potable, the countryside is invisible and the air waves unbelievable. These are the consequences of a single-minded concentration on aggregate production as a social goal. And the organizations—the great corporations—that pursue this goal increasingly see the individual as someone to be accommodated to their interest, not the reverse. If he worries about the effects of automobiles on air pollution or highways on the cities, his doubts are something not to be respected but to be overcome. He needs to be sold. Similarly as regards weapons or any lingering supposition that cigarettes cause cancer. And—an issue Ralph Nader has dramatized—if the government undertakes to regulate on behalf of the citizen, the corporations respond by regulating the regulators. Increasingly where the system does work, it does not exist for the individual. The individual and the government exist for the system.

So the old assumption of Democratic economic policy can no longer be sustained. The economic system does not work. And the reforms required to make it work—to make it work uniformly and for individuals, not the corporations—are far more fundamental than anything contemplated by the cheap and soft and easygoing liberalism of these last years. This the Party has not faced—or begun to face. I will return to these remedies presently.

III

THE FOREIGN POLICY DISASTER

THERE CAN BE NO DOUBT, foreign policy for the last fifty years has been the nemesis of the Democratic Party. Wars, just or unjust, have come with devastating reliability every time the Democrats have enjoyed power—World War I with Wilson; World War II with Roosevelt; the Korean War with Truman; the deepening involvement in Vietnam with Kennedy; and the full-scale disaster there with Lyndon Johnson. The response of the voters has been equally reliable—ignoring all affirmations of the righteousness or the inevitability of the conflict, they have thrown the Democrats out.

One afternoon in 1956, Adlai Stevenson was making the traditional pitch for the farm vote at the National Plowing Match held that year near Newton, Iowa, on the prairie between the Skunk and the North Skunk rivers. He eloquently and brilliantly dramatized the misery of farmers under the administration of Ezra Taft Benson, and the certainty that the Democrats, if returned, would satisfy their every wish. It was a highly persuasive speech, the further details of which I have forgotten, although I was the author.

When the campaign party moved on in late afternoon to Denver, I remained behind and, in the company of Donald Murphy, a sympathetic Iowa journalist, made the rounds of the assembled multitude—farm leaders, dirt farmers, barnyard philosophers—to sense the reaction. It was both favorable and devastatingly negative. None doubted that the Democrats were better for the farmer; none questioned that under the Democrats you got wars. The reply that is still singed on my mind: "My old lady still r'members Ike gottus outta Korea." Ike did. He accepted a truce that Harry Truman criticized as being the same bargain he could have had a year before. H.S.T. was criticizing the wrong man.

There have been many explanations of the popularity of Eisenhower—the war hero, the quintessential American, the father figure, the man who fitted the relaxed and unexcited mood of the fifties. Mostly, I think, he ended the Korean war on terms that a Democrat would have feared to accept lest he be accused of appeasement. When he did, his re-election in 1956 became inevitable. If this is a fair interpretation of history, one could hardly be surprised at an adverse reaction to the Democrats when, ten years later, they got the country bogged down in yet another war in another country which, given the nature of cartography, seemed only a few miles south of Korea. If the Democrats suffered for the just wars, they could hardly expect to be rewarded politically for one that a large minority of voters, and eventually a majority, came to think unwise, unnecessary or positively foolish.[3]

In past months Democrats who oppose the war have marveled at the way President Nixon has been getting away with a policy in Vietnam which all must know

[3] I am tempted to quote from a letter to President Kennedy from India in March, 1962. "I worry about Indo-China . . . it is the political poison that is really at issue. The Korean war killed us in the early '50's; this involvement could kill us now. That is what the military and the State Department will never see."

is a terrible fraud. The policy assumes that we can give a manifestly incompetent, corrupt and unpopular government enough weapons to sustain itself against both the enemy and a great many of its own people. This was something that it barely did when propped up by 500,000 Americans and Ellsworth Bunker. It implies that the most vital and durable political force in the country, the NLF, will somehow accept exclusion from power. Meanwhile the pace of withdrawal of the American forces is agonizingly slow. But my friends do not realize—nor did I for some time—that people compare Mr. Nixon's policy not with a perfect one but with what they had before. Between continued escalation under the Democrats with all its anxieties made deeper by President Johnson's oratory, and de-escalation under the Republicans, there is a difference as between night and day. Between fraudulent and well-conceived de-escalation under the Republicans, the difference is not so much.*

Thus the Vietnam adventure or misadventure as the culminating disaster of Democratic foreign policy. It does not explain why the Democrats, on many matters respected both by themselves and by others for their intelligence, got themselves into this mess. The sources of the error are worth understanding, especially if there is to be any improvement in the future. They are not simple. And while I do not belong to the school of historians which exculpates individuals on the grounds that it is impolite to assess blame, the sources of the mistakes somewhat transcend even the considerable personal responsibility of Lyndon Johnson and Dean Rusk. There is also the tendency for what is right in

* This went to press just as President Nixon ordered the invasion of Cambodia. This abject surrender to the military bureaucracy, one can only suppose, will bring the President's long period of grace on Vietnam to an end.

foreign policy at one time or place to be wrong at another time and place. This complication is less appreciated by critics on the left than might be wished.

2

The Democratic foreign policy disaster had its roots in its success following World War II and the conclusions, mostly false, that were drawn from that success. Responsibility rests also with the kind of leadership that was deemed necessary to exploit that success, and with the delegation of power that was made to it. A final cause of the disaster was the bureaucracy, military and civilian, that came into existence to conduct the foreign policy.

The success was the management of Soviet pressure on Europe in the years from 1945 to 1952. In the mature view, one can conclude that the Soviet Union, under Stalin, was then pursuing, with accustomed crudity, a militarily orthodox, highly self-centered policy. It was seeking to ensure that its western maches—the invasion routes of the armies of Napoleon, Wilhelm II and Adolf Hitler—would henceforth be covered by states that were safely subordinate to its authority and safely receptive to the presence (or return) of the Red Army. And, of course, it was concerned to ensure the reduction and neutralization of German military power, which, more than any other country except France, it had practical reason to respect. But as pursued without subtlety by Stalin, accompanied by the Communist revolution in China and orchestrated by Communist rhetoric, it was easy to imagine that this policy implied much more—that it implied a plan in process for world revolution. Among men whose fear of their God is usefully reinforced by fear for their property, alarm over atheistic Communism is easily encouraged. It can become paranoiac. There were many such in the United States at the time.

And events in Europe in the late forties could have outrun Soviet policy. They did in Greece as very possibly also in Korea. In Greece Communist pressure there in the years immediately following the war (and inspiring the so-called Truman Doctrine) was, it now appears, despite Soviet opposition, not because of Soviet encouragement. Similarly the Chinese revolution was the work of Chinese, not Russians. (Stalin, like some Americans, initially dismissed Mao as an agrarian reformer.) Had Italy and France remained economically distraught, politically disoriented and militarily a vacuum in the years from 1946 on, their large and cohesive Communist parties might have taken over—and without any particular encouragement from the Soviets. One of the errors of the period, as I shall argue presently, was in exaggerating the power of a superpower, American or Soviet, to control such events.

For better or worse—my own orthodox instinct is to think for better—this did not happen. And its failure to happen coincided with a vast and many-pronged initiative by the Democratic administration in Washington—the Truman Doctrine on behalf of Greece and Turkey in 1947, the Marshall Plan in 1948 and numerous military steps leading to the rearming of Germany and the creation of NATO in 1949.

Of these actions, the Marshall Plan made the most profound and lasting impression. Here was free enterprise, supplemented by a sizable infusion of capital, combined with sound American leadership. Something great could be expected. Expectations were justified; Western Europe came back with marvelous speed.

Whether it would have gone to the Communists without the Marshall Plan will never be known. The great fact is that with the Marshall Plan it did not.

Improved economic well-being was accompanied by greater political stability. Support for violent solutions waned. This proved what liberal Democrats had always held—and wanted to believe. Sound economic policy made sound political sense. But, additionally, the European military forces, strengthened by American aid, and the NATO forces deployed across Western Europe, helped guarantee internal tranquility as well as the frontiers. Conservatives like this kind of hard-headed, unsentimental answer to the Reds. There was something in this policy for everyone. Working so well, so brilliantly, in Western Europe, it was natural to conclude that it would work everywhere. In 1950 the Korean war made the Communist threat seem universal. So the European package—economic assistance, military support, collective resistance—became a universal answer.

3

With the policy in the late forties and early fifties went an equally precise view of the kind of men who should run it. Needed in addition to the professionals of the State Department and Pentagon were successful lawyers and businessmen, preferably liberal Republicans. In part this was to win Republican support in the Congress. This was a matter of undoubted moment between 1946 and 1948 when the Republicans, reflecting the normal reaction of the American voter to war, even a widely approved and indubitably victorious one, had control of both Houses. But even more, it was because nearly all liberal Democrats with experience of foreign policy were disqualified—or had disqualified themselves. The Roosevelt administration had been in the closest wartime association with the Soviets under Stalin; most of its members had taken the association very seriously. Some had been romantic. Now with Stalin the archenemy and the Soviet Union the international villain, those who had been so involved were not the sort of men to be entrusted with the new policy. It had better be someone whose intelligence was considerable, whose respectability was impeccable and whose anti-Communist sympathies were beyond doubt. Of such men the business community and the bar—especially the New York legal establishment—had a more than ample supply. So they—Robert Lovett, Paul Hoffman, John J. McCloy, the Dulles brothers (who began under the Democrats), William Burden, William Foster, Paul Nitze and many others—were recruited. Quite a few continued under the Republicans. In time it came to be supposed, not the least by those involved, that such men had an exclusive franchise on foreign policy.

When, in the late forties, Alger Hiss was shot down just before completing his extremely daring traverse from the fashionable left-wing establishment of the thirties to the cold-war establishment of the forties, the disqualification of those who had been associated with foreign policy under F.D.R. became nearly complete. Democrats were definitely suspect. Adlai Stevenson, who had played a minor role under Roosevelt, and Dean Acheson, who had compensated for a more important one by becoming the leading cold-war strategist, had trouble proving their eligibility. Only Averell Harriman, who had encountered liberal criticism during World War II for his highly unsentimental view of

Stalin, occupied a position of major leadership in the two periods. Intellectual guidance was provided by a younger generation of officials, mostly non-political, whose military or Washington civilian service had kept them safely away from the Russians. Out of conviction or thoughtful observation of the fate of those who had associated themselves with the earlier policy, they were adequately anti-Soviet. These men—Richard Bissel, Robert Richardson Bowie, Lincoln Gordon, Dean Rusk[4]—led the new guild of the day, the professional cold-war strategists. They worked under the general protection of the liberal businessmen and the New York legal establishment and in close association with the professionals of the State Department and Pentagon. This was a portentous development. Out of the need to appeal to the Republicans on Capitol Hill (this was the bipartisan foreign policy), and the need to break with the Roosevelt officeholders, foreign policy was delegated by the Democrats to the New York esablishment, the new scholarly strategists and the professional soldiers and civil servants.

The same leadership continued when the Democrats returned in 1961. Instead of Stevenson, Harriman or Fulbright with their Democratic Party associations, Kennedy turned for Secretary of State to Dean Rusk,

[4] Some of these, in turn, were to pay professionally for a too rigid commitment to the policy which was then so successful. Richard Bissell was the manager of the Bay of Pigs affair and left public life not long thereafter. Robert Bowie was the creator of the so-called Multinational Force—a design for giving Western Europeans nuclear arms by having them participate in a fleet manned by men of various nationalities and equipped with nuclear weapons targeted on the Soviet Union. When interest evaporated, he was left as the rather lonely defender of what erstwhile supporters were now pleased to dismiss as a somewhat ridiculous idea. Dean Rusk, faithful to the policy to the end, brought it to disaster, and his own reputation likewise, in Vietnam.

now become a paramount figure in the Establishment. The selection of Robert McNamara and Roswell Gilpatric for the Department of Defense (although neither was an enthusiastic cold-warrior) affirmed further the continuing delegation of foreign policy to businessmen and the New York Establishment. The influence of Chester Bowles in the State Department, an active Democrat who had held elective office, was quickly liquidated. Foreign policy was thus removed from the influence of party politics. All thought this good. Less celebrated was its not partial but total removal from the influence of men who had any personal stake in the future of the Democratic Party, the President apart. Historians will consider this a remarkably daring delegation of the policy which could, more than any other, destroy the Party.

With the passage of time, Democratic senators and congressmen (and eventually something close to a majority in the Senate) came to oppose the Vietnam involvement. The less politically involved men in the executive branch, especially in the State Department, remained stalwart. It was not that the Democratic senators were either more or less intelligent than Secretary Rusk and his associates.[5] It was only that they were far more sensitive to what the war was doing to the country, to the Democratic Party and, reflecting an aptitude common to elective politicians, to their own political prospects.

The divorce of foreign policy from Party responsibility was greatly strengthened by the tendency of the policy—the superpower vision and the accompanying economic and military measures to arrest the progress of Communism—to expand and empower the civilian

[5] The one senior State Department officer with a long record of active participation in Democratic politics was George Ball. He opposed the war.

and military bureaucracy. The bureaucratic consequences of seeking to be a superpower are of the highest importance and still only dimly perceived.

4

If one believes that through a combination of economic and military measures the country can greatly influence the course of events in other countries, and if one believes that in consequence of the Communist threat one should do so, then a further consequence is certain. There will be a colossal bureaucracy. And this bureacracy in turn will develop a life and purpose and policy of its own. "By its nature, bureaucracy . . . is unable to stop whatever it is doing except by drastic action applied from the outside."[6]

Specifically if it is believed that the economic and political development of Thailand can be greatly shaped by the United States and that the Thais are a natural bastion against Communism and must, poor bastards, have their future shaped, there will have to be a mission to supervise the infusion of capital that (following the Marshall Plan model) is essential for development. And there will also have to be auditors to regulate the indigenous tendencies to larceny. And there will be men in Washington to recruit, serve and regulate this mission. And there will be technicians in the field to help guide the development of industry, education and

[6] Vice-Admiral H. G. Rickover. Subcommittee of the Committee on Government Operations. House of Representatives. Admiral Rickover distinguishes public bureaucracy from private enterprise. It is not clear that large, private bureaucracies are intrinsically more flexible.

agriculture, and more supervisors in Washington. And other men will be needed in the field to collect the military, political and economic intelligence on which the policy is based, and more men will be required in Washington to digest this information and revise it as necessary to fit the Washington view. And there will have to be other men in the field to watch for subversion and to frustrate it, and more men in Washington to select, guide, equip, and cover up for these spooks. And a military mission will be needed to supervise the distribution of arms with which the Thai government, in accordance with the policy, defends itself against Communist incursion or insurrection and to train the local heroes in the use of these arms. This mission will be very, very large. So also will be the supporting and supervising bureaucracy in the Pentagon. Guiding the government of Thailand and guiding Washington on the guidance being provided to those that guide the Thais will be a sizable diplomatic staff. Explaining the various purposes of the Americans to the local citizens and explaining them away to the American press will be a considerable information organization. This also will be guided by men in Washington who will be guided from the field. All this is now true of Thailand. It is only moderately less true of many other places. The price of being a superpower is a truly huge organization. In 1939 the predecessor agencies at the Department of Defense had about 200,000 civilian employees. Last June 30 there were 1,341,587 on direct hire. Some 36,000 Americans now serve in foreign lands. Before World War II all overseas work was accomplished by 2,000 State Department officers and a handful from other agencies.

The tendency—the inevitable tendency—of any large organization, public or private, is to be authoritarian and exclusive. It pursues its purposes and minimizes outside interference, and does so not because it is wicked but because that is the nature of organization. So it was and is here. A great civilian and military machine was created. Its task was to move against Communism the world around. Its ineluctable tendency was—and remains—to take over. This machine was further protected in its exclusiveness—i.e., in its freedom from political control and responsibility—by secrecy. If one is countering Communist subversion in some foreign jurisdiction, one can plausibly ask for reticence. To debate these matters in Congress, even to allow politicians to know about the proceedings, is to expose one's hand to the other side. (If one is nurturing non-Communist politicians, reticence is also in order considering the type of talent commonly available.) It may even seem necessary to be circumspect in the information one offers to the President. Leaks occur in the White House. "There are no secrets in Washington," President Kennedy once observed, "except things I need to know." The worldwide war on Communism—the superpower mystique—meant a large bureaucracy, a powerful bureaucracy, and a bureaucracy protected in the exercise of power from political scrutiny. The party in power, after 1960 the Democrats, was responsible only for the results.

5

The results were disaster. A bureaucracy is governed not by the truth but by its own truth. It defends its truth against the reality. Those who question its truth are discounted for eccentricity, ignored for ineffectiveness or excluded for unreliability. The truth of the superpower bureaucracy and the foreign policy establishment as it had developed to circa 1960 was of an all-pervading Communist conspiracy, based in Moscow and reaching out through regional offices in Berlin, Prague, Peking, Hanoi and elsewhere to probe and then press on any weak place in the frontier. It was a vision given expression in a dozen speeches by Dean Rusk,[7] a hundred columns by Joseph Alsop and in its most precise form in the concept of the "truce line" by Walt Rostow. The Rostow truce line was the boundary dividing the Communist from the non-Communist world as it had become stabilized after World War II. It could be accepted but it must be defended. The Communists could be counted upon to test it, to try our intentions, and they must be left in no doubt. The Rostow truce line was, in many ways, the finest delineation of the bureaucratic truth.[8]

[7] "The central issue of the [world] crisis is the announced determination to impose a world of coercion upon those not already subject to it . . . it is posed between the Sino-Soviet empire and all the rest, whether allied or neutral; and it is posed on every continent. . . ." Dean Rusk. *Winds of Freedom.* Boston. The Beacon Press, 1962. p. 16.

[8] "Soviet policy appears to be based on sustained and sophisticated study of particular areas of vulnerability (e.g., northern Azerbaijan, Greece, Berlin, Indochina, South Korea) and particular types of vulnerability (e.g., the geographical position of Berlin, the shortage of local defenses against guerrilla warfare in Laos and South Vietnam).

"We cannot rule out that in the future the Communists will be prepared to assault directly the United States or other positions of evident strength within the free community. Therefore, it is a first charge on United States military policy to make such direct assault grossly unattractive and unprofitable. But a major lesson of postwar history is that United States and Allied policy must achieve, to the maximum degree possible, a closing off of areas of vulnerability, if we wish to minimize the number and effectiveness of Communist probes. It is this lesson which requires that the United States and its allies develop a full spectrum of military strength, under sensitive and flexible control, capable of covering all regions of the free world, if we

As Admiral Rickover observed, bureaucratic truth is rigid and unaccommodating. It is a battleship with heavy armor, much armament but no rudder. In those days it required reaction to seeming Communist aggression; it could not allow for the possibility that a Communist insurrection might arise from civil, not international causes; that there might be insurrection and revolt without Communists; and that the revolt might be beyond the civil and military power of the United States to suppress. Most of all, it could not admit this last—that a superpower might not, after all, have the power. Of course it could not hold that the Communists were themselves plural and divisive and that with some of them we, at a minimum, needed to be friends.

On all of these matters, bureaucratic truth, departing from truth, impelled the Democrats into deep trouble. The bureaucratic truth held that Communists being visibly wicked and having no indigenous support, Castro could easily be ousted in 1961. The truth was that he had wide support. The result was disaster at the Bay of Pigs. Bureaucratic truth held that there being civil disorder in the Dominican Republic, Communists must be the cause. Thus the massive military descent on that country to put things right. In truth it was a normal Latin American political brawl. The Communists, not existing in any important way, had to be invented after the fact. Bureaucratic truth held that Vietnam was a case of external aggression stemming ultimately from Mowcow, then Peking. And it held that the course of events in South Vietnam, no less than in Europe in

---

are to create a stable military environment and minimize the opportunity for Communist intrusions.

"It is toward this objective that we have been working over the past three years."

W. W. Rostow. *View from the Seventh Floor.* New York. Harper & Row, 1964. p. 27.

1948, could readily be influenced by American economic and military intervention. In fact Vietnamese Communism was an expression of intense nationalism. And the South Vietnamese countryside was beyond the reach of American economic and military power, however massively deployed. Thus the long-drawn-out disaster in Vietnam.

Such was the record of bureaucracy in pursuit of its own truth. Had bureaucracy been rigorously checked and corrected by strong and skeptical political leadership, perhaps the results would have been different. But the Democrats gave away the leadership too. Bureaucracies survive. So have the leaders to whom the power was delegated—although some of them have had to face temporary exile to the Old Confederacy or its environs. But the Democratic Party, with the Bay of Pigs, the Dominican fiasco and the durable and hence far more damaging disaster in Vietnam to show for its years in power, has not come off well. Nor, as one reflects, had it the right to expect otherwise.

That something went wrong in Vietnam, as also in Cuba and the Dominican Republic, is not something that any deeply percipient Democrat needs to be told. The conclusions to be drawn from these disasters —that in much of the world there is little that the United States can do and less that it should do, that a party must not delegate to the experts the power that can destroy it, that bureaucracy can be unswerving in its purposes even when these are drastically opposed to the public interest—have been less fully learned. And not learned at all is the most important lesson of all, which is that we cannot risk a foreign policy that requires large and dangerous delegation to a large military and foreign policy establishment. These are very practical matters to which I will return.

IV

THE POLITICS OF ANACHRONISM

AMONG THE GREATEST CURIOSITIES of American politics are the outlandish things that are tolerated, even praised, because they exist. Vested intellectual interest plays a role. Political comment in the United States is a considerable industry employing a sizable number of people supporting their loved ones and serving a substantial market. In the hands of some of its great practitioners—Novak, Sevareid, Crawford—it is highly automated and thus superbly predictable. But to be so, its operatives must defend those features of the political system to which they are programmed. What exists they must believe to be normal and right, however odd. Change, however logical, requires new thought. It is better dismissed as being motivated by men who do not fully respect the system.

The examples of this ability to sanctify the irrational or the obsolete are legion—congressional procedures, the seniority system, the system of financing elections, J. Edgar Hoover, many more. But the most remarkable manifestation is the ability to think of Senators John Stennis and Gaylord Nelson, and Representatives Mendel Rivers, Allard Lowenstein and John Conyers all as members of the same political party. And it is not alone the political sages who are noteworthy in this respect. The ability of liberal Democrats to accept the incredible is even more to be remarked.

The classical function of the political party is to unite men of broadly similar views who seek to undertake or influence the tasks of government. As often it brings together men of dissimilar views to effect a compromise. (Shared greed, as the late John Steinbeck averred, is nearly as beneficent an influence in the state as shared aspiration and rather more common.) But it has never been the function of a political party to bring together men of irreconcilable views—men of implacable hostility. That is what the Democratic Party now does with the further consequence of according power to an intransigent minority which would otherwise not enjoy it.

The Democratic Party encompasses the traditional southern white politicians who, with the passage of time, have come to see the primary purpose of politics as the assertion in whatever semantic disguise of traditional white supremacy and the black citizens, North and South, who, like other minorities over the years, have come to the Democratic Party because it seemed the best available instrument for advancing racial equality. Between those who are against racial equality and those they proclaim to be unequal, there is no ground for compromise.

Almost as starkly, the Democratic Party joins those, again the southerners, to whom the crisis of the modern city is a matter of indifference and the urban legislators to whom, if they are serious politicians, this is central. And it joins the martial sons of the Confederacy with the most ardent opponents of the Vietnam war. Among the processors of standard political comment there is a cliché that to find such implacable hostility within the ambit of a single political party is, by some odd manifestation of national eccentricity, peculiarly American.

This is nonsense. It is a device for keeping in power the most regressive part of the American political community.

Not for years have the Democrats functioned as a party for presidential elections. Large sections have defected routinely every four years—to Strom Thurmond, George Wallace or the Republicans. At the 1948 Convention, the strains were already sufficient to provoke a walkout by southern delegates. The error in this tactic was soon seen. They needed the Party more than the Party needed them. And this was made evident on a small scale at Atlantic City in 1964 and then on a larger scale in Chicago in 1968, with the exclusion of the racially more intransigent southern delegations. Only in the Congress does the Democratic Party ever act as a national party. This is once every two years when the Democrats vote as a party to organize the two Houses of Congress. In this ceremony the majority of the Party—the modern wing which has long monopolized the presidential power—places itself under the control of the southern wing of the Party. The control is exercised by the southern committee chairmen. Having thus empowered men whose beliefs are wholly at odds with the avowed convictions of the rest of the Party, and who represent a small fraction of its total voting numbers, the Party as a party then dissolves. The southern leaders form a coalition with conservative Republicans for the ensuing two years. The northern majority then fights the coalition for the same period. Thus the one unified *national* accomplishment of the Democratic Party is to accord power to Richard B. Russell of Georgia, John Stennis of Mississippi, Allen J. Ellender of Louisiana, James O. Eastland of Mississippi, Russell B. Long of Louisiana, John L. McClellan of Arkansas, B. Everett Jordan of North Carolina, L. Mendel Rivers of South Carolina, William M. Colmer of

Mississippi, Jamie L. Whitten of the same state, Wilbur D. Mills of Arkansas, Otto Passman of Louisiana, John L. McMillan of South Carolina and William R. Poage of Texas. All are key committee or subcommittee chairmen. By the grace of the majority with which they most devoutly disagree, these men enjoy an authority to which they could not, in any other circumstances, possibly aspire.

2

The composition of the Democratic Party was not always as wildly irrational as now. Like most obsolete arrangements it was made so by passage of time. Through the New Deal years, Negroes in the South were voiceless and politically destroyed as they had been since the collapse of Reconstruction. And northern Negroes rallied to the Democrats not on the issue of civil rights and equality, but because F.D.R. had given them jobs and social security. And if gratitude did not inspire a sufficient sense of civic duty among black citizens, the northern Democratic bosses provided the requisite additional encouragement as in some cities, notably in Chicago, they still do. So there were no issues of civil rights and social and economic equality to induce irreconcilable hostility.

There were other grounds for agreement. Agriculture was still important; there was an element of Populism in southern politics. Support for cotton, tobacco, peanuts, TVA and the textile industry could be won only by according reciprocal support of relief, welfare and even labor legislation sponsored by northern Democrats. It was an uneasy alliance, but in the main it was southerners—Joseph T. Robinson of Arkansas, Pat Harrison of Mississippi, James Byrnes of South Carolina, Lister Hill of Alabama—who guided the Roosevelt legislation through the Senate. It was also another southerner, Huey P. Long, who most ardently belabored these gentlemen (and Roosevelt) for being too conservative.

Time has totally removed this community of interest. Agriculture has declined greatly in importance. Its present legislative needs are settled by a small legislative subsystem working with the Department of Agriculture of which most members of Congress are only casually aware. Northern support is rarely needed. If it intrudes, it is likely to ask inconvenient questions about payments to large landowners or malnutrition in the southern countryside. Southern Populism has disappeared. Few southern voters are available for welfare, labor or urban legislation.

Meanwhile, blacks in the South have started to vote. Northern blacks are conscious of their identity. They are no longer grateful for economic crumbs. Neither have they anything in common with those whose purpose is to deny the black community access to economic advantages and political power. Whites who depend on black votes must be even more careful in their association. Not only is the community of interest gone, but the two sides cannot be safely seen talking to each other.

3

The disappearance of the old southern leadership is, in fact, only a matter of a few years. At the next convention, black or decently integrated delegations will present themselves from nearly all of the southern states and with a plausible claim to be seated. Northern delegations, under pressure from black members and voters, will seat them. This means that white politicians in the South who want to retain any influence in the Party will have to come to terms with the black voters. This will be true in Congressional and Senate races—a coalition of black voters and their white allies will increasingly threaten the old guard. The recent discovery by Harry Byrd, Jr., that he could not be renominated as a Democrat in Virginia, once racially among the most regressive of states, is a highly encouraging sign of the times. In the absence of some crushing setback to black voting in the South, there will be many more such enlightened discoveries in the years ahead.

Supporting and abetting this salutary trend are the Republicans. The southern strategy could not have been better timed to persuade Democratic segregationists that they have a spiritual home in the Republican Party. The inspired visibility of the Carswell and Haynsworth nominations together with the footdragging on school desegregation and voting rights have reinforced the effect. Bigotry is rarely combined with great political perception; the man who is susceptible to the slogans of white supremacy will also believe that John N. Mitchell can make him supreme.

Increasingly blacks, especially in the North, are wondering if either of the parties or the system of which they are a part will ever serve their cause. But the Republicans are ensuring that however inadequate the Democrats, none will think the Republicans any better.

4

In my view the Democrats will become better, but it would be well to expedite the process. There is black patience to be reckoned with. The most immediate need is an attack on the congressional seniority system. This is the citadel of southern white power. It will be strongly defended by those who possess the power as well as by all who cherish the world's outstanding example of planned gerontocracy. But the way is also open to liberal Democrats to end this anachronism and make honest the relation of the Party to its black members. And such a course has now been suggested by liberal members of the House of Representatives. The remedy is to vote with the Republicans next January (assuming that the Republicans need the vote) to allow them to organize the House of Representatives. Nothing is lost by exchanging conservative or reactionary Democrats for conservative or reactionary Republicans. Once lost, the traditional southern power will never again be restored. Such an action, in turn, will speed reform in Congressional and Senatorial primaries in the South. The old leaders will have to face primaries without the prestige and power (and, in the case of a man like Mendel Rivers, the considerable military patronage) of their committee chairmanships. The admirable electoral process by which they are being removed from the scene—as their segregationist supporters go to the Republicans and as black and white southerners unite behind modern men—will be expedited. It will be better for the Democrats in at least one of the Houses to be a minority party that is half-way modern than a majority party that empowers anachronism. This is not, for the Democrats, a way of giving up the South (as will be said), but of keeping it.

V

THE MATTER OF POLITICAL STYLE

"The choice between light and darkness, between health and sickness, between knowledge and ignorance is not one that we can ignore. The light that we generate can be the brightest hope of history. It can illuminate the way toward a better life for all."

Lyndon B. Johnson
February 2, 1966

AMONG THE MANY THINGS that can damage a politician, none, imaginative larceny not excepted, is so serious as being too long in office. It is why, in all well-regulated societies, those who inhabit official positions are at suitable intervals peacefully or violently expelled and replaced by equally ordinary men who, however, are much superior from not having been previously in public position. In the United States, the Democrats have been in control of the Executive for all but nine and a half of the last thirty-seven years and for most of that time they have been, though nominally, in charge of the Congress as well. The consequent damage has been very great.

This is not the corrupting effect of power. The ordinary legislator or appointive official in Washington does not have enough power to endanger even the most dangerously susceptible soul. Far, far more statesmen are corrupted each year by high-proof whisky. In any case, the frustrated yearning for power can be as debilitating as its exercise. The damage from being in office comes from three other causes. These are the endemic tendency of the officeholder to caution as exaggerated by his staff; the ghastly effect of long-continued association with bureaucratic truth; and the temptation arising from recent Democratic policy, both foreign and domestic, to hyperbolic overpromising. Each of these requires a word.

2

The impulse of the politician to guard his tongue—to hedge, evade and mumble—is as old as government itself. And it is addictive. With age the officeholder does not tend to silence, which would be tolerable. Rather he resorts to one or another of the political surrogates for substance. The greatest of these is rhetoric. In the not remote past, a few gifted practitioners—Franklin D. Roosevelt, Adlai Stevenson at his best—have been able by sheer oratorical skill to make their audience overlook the fact that the real questions were being avoided. (They were also wise enough to ration these efforts.) Their example, in turn, has encouraged a legion of road-company windbags to believe that a few memorable phrases—warnings against fearing fear itself; calls for crime, like Carthage, to be destroyed—would relieve them from the need to say anything. The Democratic Party is richly endowed with such men.

Competing with them are those that believe that an aspect of great moral earnestness is a surrogate for simple truth. Lyndon Johnson believed this deeply. Knowing that his reputation, if not for mendacity, was certainly for brilliant verisimilitude, he adopted a manner of deeply injured moral rectitude on all public occasions. This inspired real mistrust. Differing only in manner is Richard Nixon. Mr. Nixon adds a further very personal touch by proclaiming, with great sincerity, his desire to be clear just before becoming wholly unclear.

Radio and especially television have profoundly reinforced the ancient political instinct to non-speak. Error is no longer confined to the immediate audience by whom it may not be noticed, from which it may go no further or where it may be intercepted and corrected. Instead it goes more or less instantly to the world at large. The result is the prepared speech laboriously concerned with syntax, elaborately eliding thought, a variant of which is the candid, impromptu and relaxed interview in which the words and manner serve as a substitute for information. This is in the presence of television commentators who since appearance and style are the requisites are likely to be professionally unaware of the difference.

These tendencies are further refined and deepened by the need of the modern politician, the issues being numerous and complex, to rely on staff. The staff assistants of a politician are compulsive writers of historic and even deathless prose. These for them are a safe substitute for content. Only the rarest staff member encourages the latter; if he does and public retribution ensues, he is to blame. It is far safer to warn of the lurking dangers in an idea, however banal or benign. Thus he combines an impression of wisdom and prudence with the maximum of self-protection.

Time, to repeat, confirms all of these tendencies. In consequence, the longer a man has been in office, the more cautious he becomes. And the longer a party has been in office, the more cautious its style and mood. The caution communicates itself to the public increasingly as dullness or even dimness; the evasion, however disguised by rhetoric, moral purpose or soaring phrase, comes over increasingly as crap. The man is chipped away, depersonalized, and becomes a parody of himself as a politician. Eventually he adds to the effect by extolling integrity. This is why the Democrats, having been long in office, are compulsive in their praise of integrity. It's a test.

Not quite all politicians are subject to this process. More than anything else it was, perhaps, the genius of President Kennedy that he understood the danger. (I recall his preparation for an early press conference as President. Answers to the anticipated questions on foreign policy had been prepared by the State Department. All advised evasion. Presently the President reacted in anger. "I can evade questions without help; what I need is answers.") But such exceptions are rare. And in a party old to office, they are very rare indeed. Among the learned observers last year it was believed that Vice-President Agnew had struck a deep and responsive chord by his criticism of the political bias of the networks. There is another explanation. People responded with surprise and pleasure to a politician who seemed to have an opinion—even one of the Vice-President's opinions.

3

The longer men have been in office, the longer and more intimate also will have been their association with bureaucratic truth, and the more likely they will have confused this with truth. The bureaucratic truth will then also strike the ears of unconditioned listeners as nonsense and they will be repelled. This too is a price that Democrats have paid.

Away from Washington in these last years, it has seemed odd that the fate of mankind was being settled in Saigon, Hué, Vientiane and Phnom Penh. One had to believe that whoever controlled the fate of mankind was eccentric in his choice of capitals. But this was the bureaucratic truth. In Washington it replaced the truth; to believe was to be informed, sophisticated, in.

Away from Washington it was also difficult to believe that we were winning this war. One troublesome point was why each brilliant success (such as the Tet offensive) brought a request for more soldiers. But in Washington one saw men who had just been out to see Westy. And there was access through the bureaucracy at second, third or fourth hand to the latest intelligence information and the newest batch of captured documents. These affirmed the bureaucratic truth, which was that defeat, properly understood, was bringing us to the brink of victory.

Away from Washington men might wonder whether, if we did not fight in Vietnam, we would *really* have to fight on the beaches in Hawaii. In a bureaucracy one respects what the leaders say.

Away from Washington in past years, it was possible to wonder if democracy was best preserved by inviting the ultimate showdown with the Communists and accepting fifty or sixty million casualties. To a man who had associated with Curtis LeMay or Nathan Twining, this showed only a willingness to look the world in the eye.

The most remarkable political phenomenon of our time, as I have said, was the revolt against the war in Vienam and the associated if less spectacular insurrection against a military-dominated foreign policy with no outcome except a steady accumulation of ever more massively destructive weapons against the eventual day of total annihilation. It did not begin in Washington. Here men were best informed on war and the weapons race. But here association with bureaucracy had extensively professionalized attitudes toward death and nuclear destruction. They were part of the day's work. The reaction came from the country, where the dulling effect of bureaucratic doctrine had not occurred, where war and nuclear annihilation still seemed unpleasant. All who were associated with the political opposition to Vietnam noticed that Washington officialdom and its penumbra of lawyers, labor leaders and erstwhile liberals operating as corporation fixers were the very last to react. There was much anger as to what the kids, the professors and eventually the country were up to.[9] In this environment many legislators fell dangerously behind their constituents, and some later found themselves in an unseemly scramble to catch up. Washington Democrats—officials, lawyers, legislators, lobbyists—were the last of all to believe that Lyndon Johnson

[9] In a speech at the National Press Club on February 23, 1966, Mr. McGeorge Bundy said that he believed it was "wholly wrong and a great error" to conclude from the debate going on in Congress and the universities that either Congress or the academic community was against the policies in Vietnam.

could be unhorsed on the issue of the war, or that those who were making the effort were more than quixotic or less than silly.

A bureaucracy is a continuing congregation of people who must act more or less as one. Its major test of truth is forthright; it is that on which those of influence can agree. And whatever it agrees on the public is expected to accept and believe. This expectation is wildly optimistic but it is another mark of a too extended association with the bureaucracy when this is not recognized. Meeting in Washington earlier this year, the Democratic Policy Council produced what could well become a minor classic of this optimism. (I was absent from the meeting and hence can claim no credit.) Reconciling the need to denounce the Vietnam war with the discomfort of those who, while in office, had been forced to defend it, the Council resolved that "the strength of our economy, as our resources of human life and spirit, is drained by a war that has been *prolonged unnecessarily.*" (Italics added.) That the public would believe that the war became unnecessary just when the Republicans came to power (this being the agreed truth) was assumed. Most others will think it improbable.

The impact of bureaucratic truth on the man too long in office is greatest in the case of military and foreign policy. Here the pseudosophistication derived from association with generals, diplomats and spooks most radically divorces a man from reality. The domestic civilian bureaucracy being less monolithic and more closely in touch with the American public is more subject to the corrective influence of public opinion. But the domestic bureaucracy has also its peculiar truths. On economic policy, in recent years, it has been deeply committed to the homeopathy of economic expansion. Given growth and the price system, all else is good. Environmental problems are cosmetic, not systemic. Unemployment and inflation, however unpleasant for those immediately involved, are technical faults and certainly nothing to justify any interference with the free-price system. And a severe monetary policy, however unpleasant for the small-business man or would-be house owner who must borrow money, is something that should be tolerated for the common good.

Association with these truths has again dulled the reactions of Democratic officeholders. Of late there has been something of a rush in Congress to come abreast of popular concern over the environmental consequences of industrial expansion. Again it was public opinion that forced the issue. And there is still a general acquiescence in an economic policy that promises unemployment as a cure for inflation and arranges to get both. The wage and price restraints which would lessen the dependence on tight money, i.e., under the interdiction of bureaucratic truth. In foreign policy, exposure to bureaucratic truth makes a man dangerous. In domestic policy, it makes him obsolete and something of a bore.

4

Finally there has been the highly adverse effect on Democratic style of hyperbole. It is what British commentators have called Dawnism. In a society which is not without sorrow, there is a natural if adolescent tendency to hope that some new leader, some new victory, some new policy will bring the dawn of a new day. Men long in office yield to the temptation to play to such hopes. Among Democrats, the success of Keynesian and Welfare State encouraged such imagining here at home. The Marshall Plan and the superpower syndrome encouraged it on a world scale. The politician who responded established himself as a man of vision. He was not afraid to think great thoughts. With the passage of time, such thoughts cease to be a guide to intention. They become an advertisement of the capacity for unfettered thought of their author. Great vision then became a surrogate for great action or any action.

In consequence, the Democratic oratorical style in the last ten years has run increasingly to Dawnism. Lyndon Johnson was its greatest practitioner. (An example heads this chapter.) Hubert Humphrey was an apt and energetic pupil. The promises of the Book of Revelation are modest, on the whole, compared with what these two men have pictured for this planet. They offered a new Marshall Plan for Asia. Humphrey proposed another Marshall Plan to rescue American cities. There was to be a special one for the Mekong and the two Vietnams. Poverty in the United States was not to be lessened; Johnson promised its extirpation as the result of an *unconditional* (sic) war. On education, racial equality, economic opportunity, housing, nutrition and the Appalachian Plateau, the visions were almost equally boundless. Presently people who are promised everything resort to the obvious protection. They believe nothing.

This as regards the Democrats may well have happened. Richard Goodwin, the most original of observers of the American political scene, believes that Lyndon Johnson has brought Dawnism to an end. As the Vietnam war increasingly monopolized the nation's moral and physical resources and thus increasingly inactivated his administration, the President increasingly resorted to visions of the domestic and world nirvana that would come once peace was restored. The result, he suggests, was that people stopped believing public promises of any kind and now switch off the set whenever a politician starts offering any.

This may be so. Certainly all who campaigned with Eugene McCarthy noticed how well voters reacted to his refusal to promise anything including his own election. Certainly Democratic orators face an interesting problem in the months and years ahead. As part of the Johnson legacy, the more they promise the less that will be expected of them.

5

In politics, the difference between style and substance is less than sometimes supposed, for the style of a politician is often a good index of his quality. Voters in primaries will do the Democratic Party a service if they react to style in the years ahead. They should watch closely any man who has been around a long while. If the personal experience which he praises has cultivated the habits of caution, evasion and use of wordy and effusive sincerity to cover evasion, he should be thrown out. The voter should also suspect all rhetoric. Hermann Goering once said that when he heard the word "culture," he reached for his gun. There should be a similar if more peaceful reaction to the politician who is seen to be struggling for a deathless phrase.

In a world where the most important task of the legislator is to regulate and curb the power of public and private organization, nothing so disqualifies a legislator as susceptibiltiy to bureaucratic truth. Any man who returns home to explain why we are in Vietnam, Cambodia, Laos or Thailand, or the need for avoiding any action on inflation that endangers the free market, can also be safely put down as pretty far gone.

Finally all who promise change must promise it in plain and matter-of-fact language. And any man who wills the ends must specify the means. That is to say, he must explain exactly where he will get the money and how he plans to mobilize the requisite political support. No more Dawnism.

VI

THE WAY BACK

REMEDY FOR THE DEMOCRATS follows, not surprisingly, from the diagnosis. Some things are sufficiently obvious. If men suffer from having been too long in office, the answer is to end their suffering. Although in politics the one thing worse than the old fogy is the young fogy, neither is essential. In all primary elections there should be a general presumption against incumbents and it should be very strong in the case of those in whom deathless phrasemaking, other rhetorical devices for evasion, bureaucratic truth or Dawnism can, however faintly, be detected. Where, this autumn, a Republican of evident candor and honest mind is opposing a Democrat who is far gone with these flaws, it will be a service to the Democrats to support this Republican.

2

The Democrats have no choice but to accept, and then to make adequate, the guaranteed income. And they should reflect concurrently on the disastrous caution that allowed the Republicans to get this one first.

They must stop evading the issue of inflation. Where strong unions bargain with strong corporations, there will have to be controls. This doesn't interfere with the market. It restrains sensibly by public action prices that are otherwise fixed with public damage by private action.

All candidates should be asked this autumn to declare themselves on the seniority system. It can no longer be the only national purpose of the Democratic Party to empower Mendel Rivers, Jamie Whitten and their friends. If reform means voting for the Republicans in the House of Representatives, so be it. An argument can be made for keeping the Democrats in control of the Senate to keep John Mitchell's friends off the Supreme Court and because it is cautiously liberal. There is no similar case for the House.

With the end of southern rule, the Democratic Party can be unequivocal in its support of racial equality both North and South. There must be such a party. It will have pinned on it responsibility for the impatience of the black community and resulting violence. It will have to face the likelihood that, up to a certain point, progress is as likely to beget impatience and extremism as to be a solvent for it. There is no other course. The liberal answer to extremism is still to remove its cause. It is the only hope for sustaining the coalition between blacks and white liberals in the South that is now taking form. Nothing less will ensure or justify the loyalty of black support (and that of Spanish-speaking and other minorities) in the North. Every effort must also be made to keep the unions in the Party. As black workers become more numerous in the union ranks, this should become easier rather than more difficult. But no concessions can be made to backlash sentiment of white workers. Nor can the older AFL-CIO leaders be accommodated in their preference for candidates who were good in the days of F.D.R.

3

Racial equality, a phrase which comes too glibly to one's lips, means continuing and doing better the things on which equality depends—in providing full access to political life, education, employment, income, union membership, housing and the protection of law. Most of all, as a purely practical matter, it requires that the Democrats become an aggressively urban party devoted to making city life in the United States not merely tolerable but safe, healthy, prosperous and pleasant. It is in the cities that the black and Spanish-speaking minorities in overwhelming numbers live. Unless the cities are good, they cannot have a decent life. The policy should also be attractive to the considerable number of whites who still survive in the cities.

Two things are required. The first is that, having contemplated all of the other remedies for urban decay, we should now try using money. We must stop using sociology as a substitute for taxation. That ample funds for city services—for the schools, police, courts, sanitation, public transportation, parks, playgrounds, museums, public festivals—will make city life agreeable may not be clear. But financial starvation does make urban life intolerable. And good and amply financed amenities do make urban life quite tolerable for people of various races in other countries.

Modern city life is incredibly expensive. To make the necessary money available, Democrats must reject out of hand the notion that Americans are overtaxed.

They are not and will be less so when foreign policy is reduced to need. A strong urban policy must include large bloc grants from the Federal Government to the large cities. (None should go to the states, which are not in any similar need.) But the money should also be given on terms that require the cities to tax their own rich, and their own commuters more adequately than now. Before John Lindsay is given final credentials as a Democrat, he must be required to make rich New Yorkers complain more about their taxes and less about their services. It is nonsense to suppose that the world's rich cannot pay for clean streets and police that protect their variously gotten gains.

The second requirement of an urban policy is plain recognition that for the most urgently needed services of the city dweller, private enterprise does not work and never will work. This is true especially of housing construction; housing repair, rehabilitation, maintenance and management; and the provision of local, commuter and interurban transportation. For these services we now have an apologetic half-hearted socialism —rent control, rent supplements, ineffectual efforts to make landlords live up to minimium standards of decency, dreary public projects that provide shelter not homes, speeches by Nelson Rockefeller that serve, most inadequately, as a substitute for trains. The answer is to take on these tasks proudly—as the Dutch housing authorities build houses, as the Swiss run trains, as Toronto, London and Moscow run their mass transit and as we have long operated that fine old manifestation of domestic bolshevism, the TVA. The city is an intensely social institution, it should surprise no one that it can only be served on important matters by social action. The Democratic Party must henceforth use the world socialism. It describes what is needed. If there is assumed to be something illicit or indecent about public ownership, it won't be done well. And the way will always be open for still more speeches calling upon private enterprise to rise to the challenge and thus postpone all remedy.

4

The remaining issue on which the Democrats must build their strength is common to both foreign and domestic policy. That is the recapture of power from organization. In the field of foreign and military policy, we must recapture the authority that the superpower mystique gave to the defense establishment, the CIA, the defense industries and the professional foreign policy establishment. Similarly at home, the mystique of an ever-expanding production, reinforced by the beneficent doctrines of the market, led to a plenary grant of power to the producing organizations—the great corporations—to use air, water, land and space for whatever in their judgment most efficiently expanded output. Here too power must be retrieved.

The remedy, however, lies not simply in the regulation of power, which, misused, causes the public anguish. It requires that we remove the reasons for the delegation. It means a foreign policy that requires no such delegation to the Pentagon, a domestic policy that requires no such delegation to General Motors. Again let me be specific.

5

Democratic foreign policy must recognize that, henceforth, there is little the United States can do and little that it needs to do to influence the political events in Asia, Africa or Latin America. We should strongly support collective resistance to armies marching across frontiers. We should participate in the humane flow of economic assistance from rich countries to the poor. The Peace Corps and technical assistance should be available without pressure. Beyond these in the Third World, as it is called, we should do nothing. No military alliances, no military aid, no training missions, no other military missions, no counterinsurgency operations, no clandestine support to friendly governments, no plots against those that are deemed unfriendly. None of this means that all will be excellent in our absence. There will be cruel misfortune and disaster. It is only that in consequence of our presence, any disaster we now know will most likely be made worse.

If we resolve never again to intervene in Asia, Africa or South America, we must expect that some countries will go Communist or what will be so described. This on the basis of past experience may also be expected to happen if we do intervene. This likelihood must now be accepted. Democratic oratory now proclaims the unwisdom of trying to police the world. The corollary is that we accept what happens in the world. If we do not, then when some jungle or desert proclaims itself for Marx, Lenin or Mao Tse-Tung, there will be talk of the need to arrest the march of Communism or, in the absence of action, of another American defeat.

Foreign policy like politics is the art of the possible. We have learned what is not possible. We must also see that below a certain level of development it matters little either to ourselves or the Communists what a country calls itself. If a country was poor and weak before it started calling itself Communist, it will be poor and weak afterward. And it will remain so for a long time. Had Communism a formula for the magical economic and political elevation of the poor countries, it would have captured them all by now. And we would have been wrong to oppose it, for we have no formula either. In the past there has been genius of a sort in our foreign policy. It has arranged defeats in circumstances where victory was not possible and was not needed.

In the Third World, the superpower mystique was an aberration of the period following World War II. That it was an aberration is now extensively recognized; what is yet to be recognized is the need to disestablish the bureaucracy—the military and bureaucratic power—that sustained that policy. To shrink this bureaucracy, and to take full political control of what remains, is central to a new Democratic foreign policy. This will not be easy. The military, intelligence and civilian bureaucracy would not be worth worrying about if it did not have power to react in its own behalf. Abdication of world responsibility, return to isolation and invitation to Communist aggression will all be averred. There will be little mention of the disasters flowing from the past policy. There will be need for Democrats to retain a certain alertness to bureaucratic truth.

6

In foreign policy the Third World has been the area of primary disaster. On the whole, things have gone much better where Europe, Japan, the Soviet Union, even Israel and the Middle East are concerned. The reason is simple. There we have been dealing (with exceptions) with strong governments. The superpower mystique has been circumscribed by what other governments would accept. Both the power delegated to and exercised by the Pentagon and the CIA has been much less. So far as the clear and present Communist danger is concerned and for doing something about it, there would be a better case for the Green Berets in Czechoslovakia than among the Meo tribes in the mountains of Indo-China. Happily the opportunity for such enlightened effort is much less. It seeks instead the vacuum in Indo-China.

But Democrats must recognize that much of our military effort in Europe and in relation more generally to the Soviet Union serves bureaucratic, not national purpose. Troop levels and deployment in Europe are still tied to the panic fears of twenty years ago when a march westward by the Red Army seemed imminent. The ABM, the new generation manned bomber and the nuclear aircraft carriers serve not the balance of terror, but the organizations that build and operate them. And beyond the curtailment in spending, and thus in bureaucratic power, that is unilaterally possible here, are the further cuts that become possible (hopefully of weapons to the Middle East as well as strategic weapons) by agreement with the Soviet Union. Once again the purpose of this policy is not alone to save money, not alone to reduce the dangers inherent in the arms race, but also and most urgently to redeem power from the military and associated bureaucracy.

The reduced foreign policy will, of course, make it possible to be rid of the draft. This now survives only because we wish to spare well-to-do taxpayers the full cost of sustaining the army that the present policy requires. So we impose not only the discomforts and dangers, but also the pecuniary costs of that policy on the young in the form of compelled service at submarket pay scales. Not surprisingly, the policy is more popular with the old than the young.

Needless to say, the next Democratic administration and all that follow must keep the reduced foreign policy under firm *political* control. For a party to delegate to experts and members of the opposition the decisions that can destroy it is wildly unwise. This Lyndon Johnson learned or anyhow experienced. There is great safety in having a foreign policy considered in terms of what the people will accept. Such reflection is a partial antidote to action on the basis of bureaucratic truth.

7

Matching the redemption of power from the military is the need to redeem it from the civil bureaucracy and the great corporations. That is the other half of the Democratic task. Part of this task is obvious. It consists in protecting at all points the rights, immunities and liberties of the citizen in an increasingly organized world. This includes the Department of Justice. It is not my personal view that our liberties are in as much jeopardy as commonly imagined. When Americans are enslaved, it will be by someone of greater demonstrated competence than the present Republican administration. A man who can be hushed up by Vice-President Agnew or John Mitchell did not have anything to say worth hearing. But the Democrats must leave no doubt as to their determination to protect people from organization and to protect privacy from the state.

The first step in redeeming power from private corporations consists in redeeming the public regulatory agencies from their control. This—the private management of the ICC, FDA and FTC by the firms that nominally they regulate—is one of the most obnoxious scandals of our time. And Ralph Nader has shown that people are deeply sensitive to the abuse. To rescue public agencies from private control, retire their time-servers, reorganize them and give them true sovereignty for their task is thus a step of prime importance and high political yield. Required is a consolidated regulatory body for all regulated industries. Like the Courts it would then be beyond the control of any single industry. Also it takes a large public bureaucracy to police powerful private bureaucracy.

But there is a much more general delegation to the private corporation which raises the whole question of the purpose of the economic system. The question here is no longer how much, in crude terms, we produce; if this remains the objective, as all conservatives will argue, we cannot much improve on present arrangements. But that phase of our history has expired. The question now is *what* we produce and *for whom* and *on what* terms. Again let me be specific.

Present productive performance is highly uneven. It is ample or more than ample where the industry is technically powerful, has large public influence and large powers to persuade. It is poor in the public sector. It is equally bad or worse where the industry is technically weak or lacks public influence. Thus the need for balance—for vastly greater investment in urban services and for public ownership—if housing and transportation are to be tolerable. But balance also requires control of excess—of automobiles for urban use, highway construction, new gadgetry such as the SST which promise more public sorrow than private good, of disposable packaging material that is now a patina over all the land. In the past we operated on the rule that all production was good. Henceforth we must assume that any item will be subject to public discussion and action. This, it will be held, will be damaging to efficiency. That can be conceded. But crude efficiency, which is to say maximum production regardless, is no longer the goal. It is only the defense of those who don't want interference.

As production ceases to be the goal, the question of who gets the product can no longer be elided—it can no longer be agreed that this problem is solved by everyone getting more. Income guarantees are part of the answer. So is more widely shared work. So is more employment in the cilivian public services. So is a far, far better system of taxation to pay for those services. The essence of such a tax system is the principle that a buck is a buck is a buck—that however a man is enriched, whether by wages, salaries, capital gains, inheritance, gift, oil or, for that matter, theft, he pay the same tax on the same enrichment. And this tax, needless to say, must be stoutly progressive and thus deliberately egalitarian in its effect. Again it will be argued that such taxation will be damaging to incentives and thus to productivity. But productivity means production and production is no longer the goal. It will again be evident how admirably the commitment to production serves the status quo—and how wise conservatives are to defend it. But not Democrats.

The *terms* on which production proceeds are, of course, those that minimize the damage to environment—that provide for orderly and agreeable use of space,[10] prohibit the disposal of waste in the air or surrounding waters, outlaw damaging productive agents and damaging consumers' goods. Again it will be argued

[10] Socialism also raises its head here. I am persuaded that the answer to effective urban and ex-urban land management is greatly increased use of public land ownership.

that such restriction is deeply inimical to efficiency. Nothing is cheaper than to dump waste in the nearest river or to march the highways and power lines across the countryside regardless. Once again it will be seen how appeal to productivity reinforces the conservative stand. Once again the Democrats will have to face up to the question of whether they are the conservative party. If not, there isn't much choice.

VII

LAST WORD

WE HAVE COME full circle. A generation ago—thirty-four years to be exact—Keynes gave the Democratic Party its all-purpose weapon against depression and unemployment. The government intervened actively in the economy to ensure high and steadily rising production. Now the question is whether that production will suffocate us—or as a more practical matter, leave Western man locked in the ultimate traffic jam. And similarly on foreign policy. Having brought the United States out of isolation, the Democrats must now bring it out of the hands of an interventionist bureaucracy which automatically defends its own power by appealing to an obsessive fear of Communism.

As always, the solutions look unpleasantly radical. They are the solutions that the Democrats, in the years of the New Economics, almost completely abandoned. One could not fight on all fronts and Democratic economists by now yearned for respectability. So it became policy to be nice to the rich. Public ownership became all but unmentionable. Above all, the system worked. A thousand speeches a year proclaimed the affection of the Party for progressive private enterprise and its distaste for regulating, interfering, hamstringing or otherwise messing into the business of this beneficent institution. Similarly on foreign policy, the military was sacrosanct and the essence of Dean Rusk's policy was to subordinate foreign policy to military need. Thus the Democrats in their oratory and their platforms were at pains to forswear all of the lines of action that the present situation requires.

2

For American conservatives, there is a wonderfully perfect arrangement. It is to have two conservative parties. Numerous Democrats share this preference. Men who have been long in office see no reason to reject the policies that, inertia being underestimated as a political force, they believe to have kept them there. And in the Congress, as sufficiently noted, political longevity is not the only avenue to leadership, but it is the only one that is absolutely reliable. Democratic candidates have always been tempted by the doctrine that, since the left had no alternative, the smart strategy was to bid for the conservatives or anyhow the middle. Some of the men immediately around Humphrey in the last campaign were ardent exponents of this doctrine. Against this is the Harriman doctrine (for Averell Harriman), which holds that liberals, when they have no place else to go, do nothing. Thus they ensure the defeat of any Democrat who woos conservatives. The Harriman doctrine is sound but not always influential.

Nice as it would be to have two conservative parties, it won't do. There will always be nervous people who will feel that problems should be tackled even though the only available remedies—taxing the rich, nationalizing industries, regulating private enterprise, limiting consumption, redeeming power and policy from military and civilian bureaucracy—are outrageously radical. The function of the Democratic Party, in this century at least, has, in fact, been to embrace solutions even when, as in the case of Wilson's New Freedom, Roosevelt's New Deal or the Kennedy-Johnson civil rights legislation, it outraged not only Republicans but the Democratic establishment as well. And if the Democratic Party does not render this function, at whatever cost in reputable outrage and respectable heart disease, it has no purpose at all. The play will pass to those that do espouse solutions—or in frustration espouse violence as a substitute. It may not immediately win elections with a radical economic policy—for radical is how it will seem, how it will be described and, in the sense that it deals with causes, what it will be. For a while longer, in accordance with American tradition, the more fortunate or sanguine will imagine that these problems—inequality, unequal economic performance, dependence on military spending and subordination to military power, industrial arrogance and environmental damage—will yield to hot air, or like Marx's state, given time, wither away. If something drastic must be done, let there be an affirmation of the ultimate workability of the system, a warning of the dangers of violence and, if things are really urgent, a call for a day of prayer. But in the end reality imposes itself. The system is not working. Violence is a threat, not a solution. The only answer lies in political action to get a system that does work. To this conclusion, if only because there is no alternative conclusion, people will be forced to come. Such is the Democratic opportunity. Oddly, I do not think the prospect entirely bleak.